Mo Dog Stories

A Dolch Classic Basic Reading Book

by Edward W. Dolch and Marguerite P. Dolch

illustrated by Meryl Henderson

The Basic Reading Books

The Basic Reading Books are fun reading books that fill the need for easy-to-read stories for the primary grades. The interest appeal of these true stories will encourage independent reading at the early reading levels.

The stories focus on the 95 Common Nouns and the Dolch 220 Basic Sight Vocabulary. Beyond these simple lists, the books use about two or three new words per page.

This series was prepared under the direction and supervision of Edward W. Dolch, Ph.D.

This series was revised under the direction and supervision of Eleanor Dolch LaRoy and the Dolch Family Trust.

SRA/McGraw-Hill
A Division of The **McGraw·Hill** Companies

Original version copyright © 1958 by Edward W. Dolch.
Copyright © 1999 by SRA/McGraw-Hill. All rights reserved.
Except as permitted under the United States Copyright Act, no part of this publication may be reproduced or distributed in any form or by any means, or stored in a database or retrieval system without prior written permission from the publisher.

Printed in the United States of America.

Send all inquiries to:
SRA/McGraw-Hill
250 Old Wilson Bridge Road, Suite 310
Worthington, OH 43085

ISBN 0-02-830811-5

1 2 3 4 5 6 7 8 9 0 BUX 04 03 02 01 00 99 98

Table of Contents

Dinner Time 5
A Funny Helper 8
Ham, for Hamburger................................. 11
Lost on the Mountain 14
Porthos, the Saint Bernard 17
Jokko 20
The Dog and the Farmer 23
Scruffy, the Movie Dog 26
Woof 32
Lady 36
Pierrot 40
Rex, a Police Dog 45
To Catch a Robber 48
Pickpocket 52

Dinner Time

He never had a name. He was just called "Dog." Dog did not carry a watch, but Dog could tell time. Dog could not tell what day it was, but Dog knew the day that Train No. 15 stopped.

Train No. 15 went through a little town in Mississippi at 6:30 in the evening. The train stopped a little while and then went on its way.

Train No. 15 carried a dining car where people sat at little tables and had good things to eat.

The cook on this train liked dogs. When the train stopped and the cook saw a hungry dog, he always gave the dog something to eat.

One day, the cook saw Dog waiting at the station. Dog always looked hungry because Dog did not have a home. The cook gave Dog something to eat.

The next day Dog was waiting at the station at 6:30 for Train No. 15, but the train did not stop at the little town that day.

The next day Dog was waiting again at the station at 6:30. Train No. 15 stopped. Dog was waiting right where the dining car stopped. The cook gave Dog something to eat. From that day, Dog waited for Train No. 15.

Dog learned not to go to the train station on the days that Train No. 15 did not stop. On the days that the train did stop, Dog was always there. Dog sat beside the dining car barking and wagging his tail.

The cook would open the little door in his car and say, "Dog, here is your dinner."

For five years, Dog did not miss meeting Train No. 15. When the sun was out, Dog was there. When the rain was falling, Dog was there. All the people who worked on the train knew Dog.

One day there was a new cook on Train No. 15. When the train stopped, Dog was there. He barked and wagged his tail, but the cook did not open his little door.

The people who were eating in the dining car looked out the windows. They asked the conductor, "What is the matter with that dog?"

The people who worked in the dining car went to the new cook. "You must give Dog something to eat," they said.

"I have better things to do," said the new cook.

Then the train conductor went to the new cook.

"The old cook has been feeding this dog for five years," the train conductor said. "Dog waits for his food every time we stop. You must give Dog his dinner."

And so the new cook gave Dog his dinner. Then Train No. 15 went on its way.

Dog went on waiting for Train No. 15 for ten years, and the cooks on the train fed Dog when the train stopped at the station.

A Funny Helper

Don was a little, black-and-white dog. He lived on a farm. Of all the animals on the farm, Don liked best a big, white hen.

At first, Don would run after the hen and bark. But the hen never seemed to be afraid of the little dog. Sometimes Don would take food away from the big, white hen. All the hen would do was "cluck" at the dog in the most friendly way.

At last, Don and the big, white hen were good friends. Don and the hen would sit side by side in the sun.

One day the hen stayed in the barn. She did not come out to sit in the sun with the little dog. Don looked and looked for his friend. He found her in the barn sitting on a nest of eggs.

Don tried in every way to get the big, white hen to play with him, but the hen just sat on her nest.

Because the hen would not come out of the barn, Don stayed in the barn and sat beside the hen. Every day for three weeks, the little dog went to the barn and sat beside his friend.

Then the big, white hen had a lot of little baby chickens. Some of the chickens were white and some were black, and some were yellow. Don liked the little chickens and tried to help the hen look after them.

If one of the little chickens got too far away from the mother, Don would make it go back. He seemed to know that the little chickens must stay with their mother.

When the big, white hen took her little family to the yard to hunt bugs, Don went along to help.

The hen said, "Cluck! Cluck!" and scratched in the dirt. Don watched the chickens hunt for bugs. Then he tried to help. Don scratched a hole in the ground. The dirt fell on the little chickens and they ran to their mother.

But the mother hen said, "Cluck. Cluck." She took the chickens to the hole that Don had made. They found many bugs. Then Don scratched another hole for the chickens.

It was very funny to watch the little dog help the mother hen look after her baby chickens. Don was a good helper.

Ham, for Hamburger

Jerry worked at a drive-in restaurant. When a car stopped at the drive-in and honked, Jerry went out to see whether the people in the car wanted a hamburger or drinks. Jerry knew that people did not like to wait for what they wanted. He was always quick to get to the cars.

One day it was raining. There was not much going on at the drive-in. Jerry was talking to the cook. The cook was making hamburgers for a man and woman who had just come in out of the rain. Suddenly, there was the sound of a horn honking outside.

"See what the people want," said the cook.

Jerry put on his raincoat and went out into the rain. He was gone a long time. When he got back, he said to the cook, "I went all around the drive-in. The only car out there is the car that belongs to these people in here who are eating hamburgers."

Jerry took off his raincoat.

Suddenly a horn honked again. It kept on honking.

Jerry put on his raincoat and went out. There was only one car outside and that was the car of the people in the restaurant who were eating hamburgers. Jerry stood and looked around. A horn honked. It was the horn of the car that was standing there. The horn honked and honked.

Jerry looked into the car. A little dog was honking the horn.

Jerry laughed. "I think you want a hamburger," he said.

Just then the man and woman came out of the drive-in. The woman was carrying a hamburger. They got into the car. Then they gave the hamburger to the little dog.

"So that is why he honked the horn," said Jerry. "He wanted a hamburger."

"Yes," said the woman, "we call him Ham, for hamburger. We always take him with us in the car. When we stop at a drive-in for a hamburger, we always have to get him one."

Jerry went back into the drive-in. He took off his raincoat. He said to the cook, "I have just been talking to Ham, a dog. He thinks you make very good hamburgers."

Lost on the Mountain

Eddie was six years old. He loved to go with his mother and her friends to pick berries on the mountain.

There were no children for Eddie to play with, but he had a big dog with him that he called Doggie. Eddie and Doggie had a good time playing together on the mountain while his mother and her friends picked berries.

When it was time to go home, Mother called Eddie. Eddie did not come. Mother and her friends hunted for Eddie. But they could not find Eddie and Doggie.

Mother stayed on the mountain. One of her friends went home as fast as she could. She told Father that Eddie was lost on the mountain. Mother, Father, and some neighbors hunted all night for Eddie.

In the night, a bad storm came over the mountain. The wind blew and rain came down. It was such a bad storm that Mother, Father, and the neighbors had a hard time getting home.

The wind blew and the rain came down all the next day. Again the people hunted on the mountain, but no one could find Eddie.

The next night, the wind and the rain stopped. In the morning, two days after Eddie was lost, a hunter came down from the mountain. He was carrying Eddie, and Doggie was walking beside him.

Mother and Father were so happy that they could hardly talk. But after a while, they asked Eddie what had happened to him.

"I found a little hole in the rocks to play in," said Eddie. "Then the rain started. It was cold, but Doggie kept me warm. Then I got hungry and went out and found some berries. I ate a lot of them, but Doggie did not like berries."

The hunter said, "When I found them, the dog would not let me get near the boy. He barked and growled. But I called to the boy, and he came to me. Then the dog wagged his tail. I gave the boy and the dog something to eat. The dog would not eat anything until after the boy ate. That dog loves your boy."

Eddie had been out on the mountain two days and two nights with only the dog to look after him.

Porthos, the Saint Bernard

Porthos was a Saint Bernard. A Saint Bernard is a very, very big dog. Porthos never got over wanting to play with toys. When he went for a walk, he always stopped to look into the window of a toy store.

Sometimes Porthos would see a toy that he wanted very much. He would sit down in front of the store window and wait. Porthos's owner would call, "Come, Porthos, come." But Porthos would just sit in front of the toy store window.

His owner would have to go into the toy store. The man in the toy store would ask, "How old is the child for which you want to buy this toy?"

Porthos's owner would say, "I want to buy a toy for that great big dog who is looking in your window." She would go to the window and point to one toy after another. When she pointed to the right toy, Porthos would bark, and she would buy that toy.

Porthos liked dolls best of all. He learned that dolls came in packages. He learned to open any package he would find. The big dog thought that every package would have a doll in it.

Porthos and his owner had fun together. They would play at fighting and would fall on the grass. But the big dog never hurt his owner.

One time, Porthos was in a play. His owner had made a play for the children. She made a part in it for Porthos.

In the play, a little girl went to school, and Porthos went to school with her. Of course, the little girl had a little cake in her pocket. Later, she would give the cake to Porthos.

The children thought the play was wonderful. When the play was over, Porthos came out with the others. He wagged his tail and barked.

Jokko

Two ladies lived in a little, white house. Mary was the older. She could not hear at all, but her quick eyes took in everything around her. Ruth was getting so that she could not hear. She knew that before long she would not hear anything.

Ruth did not know what the two ladies would do when they could not hear. They did not have enough money to have someone look after them. And they did not want to leave their little, white house in which they had lived so many years.

A kind man named Mr. Jones lived next door to the two ladies. Mr. Jones trained dogs. One day he said to Ruth, "I think that you and Mary need a dog to look after you."

Mary and Ruth were very happy. Jokko was a good helper. He would tell them when anyone was at the door. If he heard the bell, he would stand in front of them and bark. Then they would go to the door.

One day Jokko barked and barked. Ruth went to the door, but no one was there. Still Jokko barked and barked. He went first to Ruth and then to Mary.

"I do not know what Jokko wants," said Ruth.

"He is trying to tell us something," said Mary. "You had better go and get Mr. Jones. He will know what Jokko wants."

When Mr. Jones came, Jokko barked in front of him. Then he ran to the cellar door and barked and barked.

"He wants me to go down into the cellar," said Mr. Jones.

Mr. Jones went down into the cellar. And there he saw that a gas pipe was broken. People could not have known that the pipe was broken because the gas did not have much of a smell. But a dog could smell it.

"Jokko has saved your lives," said Mr. Jones.

The Dog and the Farmer

One winter a little, black-and-white dog went to a farm in Canada. No one wanted the little dog, but the farmer let him stay in the barn.

One day, when the winter snow covered everything, the farmer had to go to town to get some hay for her animals. She put a hayrack on a sled. A hayrack is a kind of big box for hay. There were two big horses to pull the sled and hayrack. The farmer stood in the hayrack and drove the horses.

The wind was blowing very hard. It was very cold. The snow was blowing so the farmer could not see where she was going. But the farmer was sure that the horses would find the way to town.

The wind began to blow harder. It blew so hard that suddenly the hayrack went off the sled. The farmer found herself in the freezing snow with the hay and the hayrack over her, and she could not get out.

The farmer tried and tried to make a hole in the side of the hayrack, but the boards were too strong for her to break. She could not break them by herself.

The farmer was still near the house. She called and she called, but no one heard her.

The cold was making the farmer sleepy. She knew that if she went to sleep, she would freeze. So she called and called.

At last, the farmer looked between the boards of the hayrack and saw a little dog running across the snow. It was the dog that stayed in the farmer's barn.

The dog came up to the hayrack that was over the farmer. He barked and barked. Then the little dog seemed to know just what to do.

The dog started to chew a hole in one of the boards. He chewed and he chewed. At last he had made a hole in the board.

The farmer was glad to see the dog. She kept saying, "Good dog. Good dog."

When the hole was big enough for the farmer to get her hand into it, she found that she could break the board. Then the farmer could get out.

The farmer was nearly freezing. She was so cold that she could hardly walk. She wanted to sit down and rest, but the little dog would not let the farmer sit down. The farmer kept walking toward the farm.

At last the farmer got home. The dog had saved her. Now the little dog has a home. He lives with the farmer and her family.

Scruffy, the Movie Dog

One day a puppy got lost. He was picked up and taken to the Home for Lost Dogs. No one came to get the puppy, so he grew up in the home.

One day a man and a woman came to look at the dogs in the home. When the woman saw this dog, she said, "That is the dog we want for the movie. He is so scruffy."

And that is how Scruffy got his name.

Scruffy's owner, Mr. Kim, helped make movies. Scruffy tried to do everything Mr. Kim told him to do. He liked Mr. Kim very much.

In making a movie, Mr. Kim could not speak to Scruffy, so Mr. Kim taught Scruffy to obey when he moved his hand. Scruffy would sit or stand or come or bark when Mr. Kim moved his hand.

One day Mr. Kim heard that a dog was needed for a part in a very big movie. Mr. Kim knew that Scruffy would be a very good dog for the part. Mr. Kim was sure that if he could get the director of the movie to see Scruffy, he would let Scruffy play the part.

Mr. Kim took Scruffy to the door of the director's office. He put out his hand and Scruffy knew that he was to "stay." Scruffy stayed by the door of the director's office all day.

Everyone who went past the office stopped to talk to Scruffy. "What a good dog," they said. "He would be a good dog to have in a movie."

But the director of the movie did not see Scruffy. The director was home, sick in bed.

Later on, Mr. Kim took Scruffy to the director's office again, but he did not get to see the director right away. So, Mr. Kim went away from the door to talk with friends. He did not see that Scruffy did not go with him.

Scruffy sat beside the door of the director's office. When someone came out of the office, Scruffy went in.

There was a man looking at some papers. He did not see Scruffy.

"Shut the door," said the man. Scruffy, who knew how to shut doors, shut the door. Then he sat beside the man, but the man still did not see him.

"Wait just a minute," said the man, "until I look over this paper."

Scruffy sat still. Mr. Kim had taught him to be still and quiet when he was told to "wait."

"Did you bring that paper?" asked the man, putting out his hand without looking up.

Scruffy knew what to do when someone put out his hand. Scruffy put his paw in the man's hand.

The man was so surprised to find a paw in his hand that he jumped out of his chair. "How did you get in here?" said the man.

Scruffy barked. And then he sat up and begged.

"Down," said the man.

Scruffy lay down on the floor beside the man's chair.

There was a knock on the door.

"Be still," said the man. Scruffy did not make a sound.

"Come in," said the man.

Mr. Kim came in. He did not see Scruffy.

"I heard that you need a good dog for the new movie," said Mr. Kim. "I think that I have just the dog that you want."

"I have the dog I want," said the director. "You must see him. He is just the right dog for the part."

"Come here," said the director. And Scruffy came out from behind the chair.

And that is how Scruffy got the part in the movie.

Woof

Woof was a very little dog with a very big bark. Woof was so little that he could ride in the pocket of his owner's great coat.

Mr. James went to Alaska to take pictures of animals, and he took Woof along. They went to live with a man in a little house in the woods. When the man saw Woof, he laughed and laughed.

"What a dog to bring to Alaska!" he said. "We have big dogs in Alaska."

In the little house and in the woods, there were many new things for Woof to see and to smell.

At night, Woof could hear the bears growl as they fished in the river near the little house. Woof was not afraid of bears.

One morning Woof and Mr. James went to the river. A bear was fishing, and Mr. James wanted to take his picture.

Woof had never seen a bear before. He ran right up to the bear that was fishing. He barked and barked and barked. The bear was sure that all animals would run away from him. But Woof did not run away. He barked and barked.

The bear looked at the dog. The bear growled. The dog barked. Then the bear turned and walked away.

One day Mr. James and Woof found a beaver working on a beaver dam. The beaver was making the dam higher. Woof had never seen a beaver before. He ran out on the dam. He fell into the water, and Mr. James had to pull him out of the water. He put Woof in his pocket to get warm and then took some pictures.

The most fun that Woof had was trying to catch a salmon.

There were many salmon going up the river. There was a place where the fish had to jump over some sand. Sometimes a salmon would jump but come down on the sand.

Woof would run out on the sand and try to hold on to the salmon by the tail. Woof pulled and pulled, but the salmon was so big and strong that it would pull Woof right into the river.

Then Woof would let go of the salmon and try to get back to the sand. Sometimes Mr. James had to pull him out of the river and put him in his pocket to get warm.

The man who lived in the little house thought that Woof fighting with the salmon was very funny.

"That little dog is not afraid of anything," he said. And the Old Man would give Woof some good things to eat.

Lady

Lady belonged to Miss Jarvis. Lady and Miss Jarvis lived in an old house in a little town. Everyone in the town knew Miss Jarvis, and everyone knew Lady.

Miss Jarvis was quite old, but every afternoon she went for a walk with Lady. Miss Jarvis walked slowly as Lady ran up and down. One day, as they were going across a street, a car hit Lady.

Lady was badly hurt. The man in the car took Lady and Miss Jarvis to the veterinarian, a dog doctor.

Dr. Ford was a good veterinarian. She took good care of Lady, and Lady got well.

Miss Jarvis was very happy to have her dog well again. She had been afraid when the car hit Lady.

"Lady," said Miss Jarvis, "I will have to take care of you. I will have to put a collar and a leash on you when we go for our walk in the afternoon."

Lady did not like to walk on a leash. She would pull and pull, and little Miss Jarvis had a hard time keeping up with her. But every afternoon they took their walk.

One day Lady was playing in the backyard of the old house. She found something in the yard to eat. It was something that made her sick. When it was time for dinner, Lady did not want to eat anything.

"What is the matter, Lady?" said Miss Jarvis. "You are always hungry for your dinner."

Lady just had a little water. Then she asked to go outside.

After a time, Miss Jarvis went to the door and called, "Lady, Lady, come in."

But Lady did not come. It began to get dark. Miss Jarvis called again and again, "Lady, Lady." But Lady did not come.

Miss Jarvis thought of how the car had hit Lady. She was afraid that Lady had been hurt again.

Miss Jarvis went and asked the neighbors whether they had seen Lady. But no one had seen Lady. Then Miss Jarvis went back to her own house and waited. Where was Lady? What had happened to her? How could she be found?

At last Dr. Ford, the veterinarian, called up.

"Is this Miss Jarvis?" said the doctor. "I just want to tell you that Lady is with me. She came to my door and barked. When I let her in, she seemed to be sick; so I gave her some medicine and put her to bed. She will be all right in the morning."

"Lady is a smart dog," said Miss Jarvis. "She was sick and she went to the doctor to get some medicine to make her well. Thank you, Dr. Ford, for looking after my dog."

Pierrot

Pierrot was a white dog who fooled his owner. Pierrot was very smart.

Pierrot may have thought that it was all right to fool his owner because his owner sometimes fooled him.

Pierrot liked to play with a white ball. His owner, Mr. Kingsley, would throw the ball and Pierrot would go and find it. Sometimes Mr. Kingsley liked to fool Pierrot. He would throw with his arm but not let go of the ball. Then he would put the ball into his pocket.

Pierrot would hunt and hunt, but he could not find the white ball. Mr. Kingsley thought this was fun, but Pierrot did not.

One day Mrs. Kingsley was fixing two chickens for dinner. She put the chickens on the table and went away for a minute. When she got back, one of the chickens was gone. She could not find it anywhere.

Who could have taken the chicken from the table?

Mrs. Kingsley went to Mr. Kingsley to tell him what happened. Pierrot was sleeping in a chair.

"I think that Pierrot took a chicken from the kitchen table," said Mrs. Kingsley.

Mr. Kingsley looked at Pierrot in the chair. "Pierrot," asked Mr. Kingsley, "did you take a chicken from the kitchen table?"

Pierrot opened his eyes. He jumped from the chair. He was very sleepy. His eyes seemed to say, "Why did you wake me? Do you want to play ball?"

"Pierrot," said Mr. Kingsley in a very hard voice, "did you take a chicken from the kitchen table?"

Pierrot hung his head.

"Look at him," said Mrs. Kingsley. "I know that he took the chicken, but what did he do with it?"

"Pierrot," said Mr. Kingsley, "where is the chicken?"

Pierrot did not move. He only hung his head.

Mr. Kingsley wanted to be sure that Pierrot had taken the chicken. He went into the kitchen and got the other chicken. He called Pierrot.

"Pierrot," said Mr. Kingsley, "here is another chicken for you."

Pierrot did not want to take the chicken, but Mr. Kingsley made the dog take the chicken in his mouth.

Mr. Kingsley had never given Pierrot a chicken before. The dog knew that something was the matter. He did not know what to do with the chicken. Slowly Pierrot went out into the garden, carrying the chicken in his mouth. Mr. and Mrs. Kingsley watched to see what he would do with it.

Pierrot put the chicken on the ground and began to dig a hole. Just as the dog was going to put the chicken into the hole, Mr. Kingsley said, "Pierrot, let me see what you have in the hole."

In the hole Mr. Kingsley found the first chicken that Pierrot had taken.

Mr. Kingsley said, "Pierrot, you are a bad dog for taking the chicken from the table. You must never take a chicken again."

Then Mr. Kingsley got some feathers from the chickens. He tied them to a stick. When Pierrot asked to play ball, Mr. Kingsley first showed him the chicken feathers. Pierrot hung his head. Then Mr. Kingsley said, "No, we are not going to play ball."

After doing this for many days, Mr. Kingsley said, "Pierrot, I think that you will never take a chicken again. Now let us play ball. I will throw the white ball for you. But I will never try to fool you again."

Rex, a Police Dog

Rex was a police dog. Rex lived in London, England. Arthur Holman, who was a police officer, trained him. Arthur Holman was a very good dog trainer, too.

Rex learned to heel, to sit, to speak, and to come. He learned what "good dog" means. Most of all, he learned "no."

Rex could track. One time a father could not find his little girl. So he called the police and told them that his little girl was lost. The police took Rex to help them find the girl.

Rex smelled a dress that the little girl had worn. Then he was told to track. Rex started off into the little town where the girl lived. He followed the smell that he found along the way.

Rex stopped to look into the windows of a toy store. He stopped at a candy store. Then he went back to the house where the little girl lived and stopped at the back door.

The police thought that Rex had made a mistake so they tried again. Again they had Rex smell the dress. Again he went to the candy store and the toy store. Again he went back to the back door of the man's house.

The police did not know what to think. They thought that maybe Rex had made a mistake. Then one police officer asked the father whether he had looked for the little girl in his own house.

The father went into the house and found the little girl sleeping in her bed.

Another time, a woman who had been taking a walk had her purse taken. The man who took her purse ran away.

The police took Rex to the place where this had happened. Rex had been taught to fetch, which means "to get." Mr. Holman told Rex to fetch. Rex looked all around on the ground. He found a button that had been pulled from a raincoat. Rex took the button to Mr. Holman.

That night, the police found a man in the street who had lost a button from his raincoat. The button Rex had found had come from that raincoat. The man said that as he ran away with the purse his raincoat had caught on something. The button had come off.

Rex had helped catch a robber.

To Catch a Robber

The police would call Rex and Mr. Holman at any time of the day or night. Many of the calls were at night. People cannot see well at night, but a dog can track at night by smelling.

One Sunday evening, Rex was called to help the police.

A neighbor had seen two men leave a house carrying sacks full of something. The neighbor knew that the man who lived in the house was away. So the neighbor called the police.

When Rex got to the house, he picked up the smell of the robbers. Away he went through the garden and down the street. The police officers could not keep up with him. Then they heard him barking.

When the police officers got to Rex, they found that he was barking at a car that stood at the side of the street. In the car, the police officers found the sacks of things that had been taken from the house. But the robbers were not there.

Arthur Holman, Rex's owner, told Rex to find them. Then he took Rex all around the car so that Rex could pick up the smell of the robbers again. Then Rex went down the road. At last Rex stopped at a bus stop, and sat down and barked. He was telling his owner that the robbers had got on a bus, so Rex could not smell them.

The robbers seemed to have gotten away. The police did not know what to do.

Just then the police were told that a man in the next town said his car had been stolen. It was the car the police had been looking at. It was the car the robbers had used. And the next town was the town to which the bus had gone.

Arthur Holman was a smart police officer. He thought, "Something is not right about this. I am going to the next town and see this man." So he told the police in the next town to keep the man for a while.

Mr. Holman took Rex with him to the next town, but he did not take Rex with him into the police station to see the man.

The man told Mr. Holman that he had been to the movies and when he came out, his car had been stolen.

Mr. Holman looked at the man's hands. They were very dirty. Mr. Holman did not think that a man would go to the movies with such dirty hands. So he called for Rex.

As soon as Rex got into the police station, he ran at the man. He knew that the man's smell was the smell of the robbers that he had tracked.

The man was afraid of Rex, so he told the police that he was one of the robbers. He had thought if he said that his car was stolen they would never think that he had used it for the robbery. But he did use it and Rex knew it.

Pickpocket

There was once a little puppy that no one wanted. His brothers and sister were big and strong. They grew and grew. They all went to good homes because people wanted strong puppies. No one wanted the littlest puppy.

The littlest puppy followed people along the street of his town. He wanted to find someone who would give him a good home. But no one wanted the littlest puppy.

One day the puppy went into Mother Murphy's store. Mother Murphy was very kind, and she let the littlest puppy sleep in the store. After that, the puppy thought he belonged to Mother Murphy. He made Mother Murphy's store his home.

The puppy grew up to be a good-looking dog, but he was never very big. He had a good home, and he liked to show how much he loved Mother Murphy. But he still followed people along the streets of his town.

One day the dog followed a little boy into a candy store. The boy gave the man a quarter and asked for a dime's worth of candy. The man gave the boy the candy and a nickel and a dime change. The boy put the change into the pocket of his coat and went out of the store.

The boy went down the street, eating the candy. The dog followed him. He begged and begged, but the boy would not give him any candy.

Then the dog jumped up and stuck his nose into the boy's pocket. He got the nickel and dime in his mouth and ran as fast as he could to the candy store. He put the money on the floor and wagged his tail.

The man in the candy store had been standing in the door of the store watching the boy and the dog.

"You little pickpocket," said the man. "The boy would not give you any candy, so you took the money out of his pocket."

The man took the dime off the floor and gave the dog some candy. Then the dog picked up the nickel and ran home to Mother Murphy.

The man at the candy store told other people about the dog who was a pickpocket. The people all laughed and called the dog Pickpocket.

Pickpocket still followed people on the street, but he begged for money, not candy. Pickpocket had found that he could buy what he wanted with money.

The people thought this was all great fun. They would give Pickpocket some money to see what he would do with it. Sometimes he went to the butcher and put a dime on the floor. The butcher gave him some meat. Sometimes he took his money to buy cake from the grocer. And sometimes he got candy at the candy store.

The people would give the little dog a quarter and a dime and a nickel to see what he would do. Pickpocket carried the money in his mouth. He went to a store where he wanted something and put the money on the floor. But he would let the owner take only one piece of money. If the owner took the quarter, Pickpocket barked until he got some change.

Pickpocket sat in the store and ate what he got. Then he picked up his change and ran home to Mother Murphy. Mother Murphy had put a little box beside Pickpocket's bed, and Pickpocket kept his money in the box.

Sometimes people on the street would not give Pickpocket any money when he begged. They wanted to see whether he would go to Mother Murphy's and get money out of his box. But Pickpocket never took money out of his box. The money in the box was for Mother Murphy. It was for her to use.

Mother Murphy was getting very old. One day she got sick and had to go to bed. There was no one to look after her but Pickpocket. Mother Murphy would write a note on a paper and give the paper to Pickpocket. Then the dog took it to a neighbor who did what the note asked.

The butcher took meat to Mother Murphy. He took his money out of Pickpocket's box. The grocer took bread and eggs. He took his money out of Pickpocket's box. When the doctor went to see Mother Murphy, he took his money out of Pickpocket's box, too.

Pickpocket looked after Mother Murphy until she died. Then many people wanted to give Pickpocket a home, but Pickpocket would not leave Mother Murphy's store. He lived there until he died.

a	barked	bugs
about	barking	bus
across	barn	but
afraid	be	butcher
after	bear	button
afternoon	bears	buy
again	beaver	by
Alaska	because	cake
all	bed	call
along	been	called
always	before	calls
am	began	came
an	begged	can
and	behind	Canada
animals	bell	candy
another	belonged	cannot
any	belongs	car
anyone	berries	care
anything	beside	carried
anywhere	best	carry
are	better	carrying
arm	between	cars
around	big	catch
Arthur	black	caught
as	blew	cellar
ask	blow	chair
asked	blowing	change
at	board	chew
ate	boards	chewed
away	box	chicken
baby	boy	chickens
back	boy's	child
backyard	bread	children
bad	break	cluck
badly	bring	coat
ball	broken	cold
bark	brothers	collar

come
conductor
cook
cooks
could
course
covered
cried
dam
dark
day
days
did
died
dig
dime
dime's
dining
dinner
director
director's
dirt
dirty
do
doctor
dog
Doggie
dogs
doing
doll
dolls
Don
door
doors
down
Dr.
dress

drinks
drive
drove
eat
eating
Eddie
eggs
end
England
enough
evening
every
everyone
everything
eyes
fall
falling
family
far
farm
farmer
farmer's
fast
father
feathers
fed
feeding
fell
fetch
fighting
find
first
fish
fished
fishing
five
floor

followed
food
fool
fooled
for
Ford
found
freeze
freezing
friend
friendly
friends
from
front
full
fun
funny
garden
gas
gave
get
getting
girl
give
given
glad
go
going
gone
good
got
gotten
grass
great
grew
grocer
ground

growl	homes	know
growled	honked	known
had	honking	ladies
Ham	horn	lady
hamburger	horses	last
hamburgers	house	later
hand	how	laughed
hands	hung	lay
happened	hungry	learned
happy	hunt	leash
hard	hunted	leave
harder	hunter	let
hardly	hurt	like
has	I	liked
have	if	list
hay	in	little
hayrack	into	littlest
he	is	live
head	it	lived
hear	its	lives
heard	James	London
heel	Jarvis	long
help	Jerry	look
helped	Jokko	looked
helper	Jones	looking
hen	jump	lost
her	jumped	lot
here	just	loved
herself	keep	loves
higher	keeping	made
him	kept	make
his	Kim	making
hit	kind	man
hold	Kingsley	man's
hole	kitchen	many
Holman	knew	Mary
home	knock	matter

may	nest	packages
maybe	never	paper
me	new	papers
means	next	part
meat	nickel	past
medicine	night	paw
meeting	nights	people
men	no	pick
minute	nose	picked
miss	not	Pickpocket
Mississippi	note	Pickpocket's
mistake	now	picture
money	obey	pictures
morning	of	piece
most	off	Pierrot
mother	office	pipe
mountain	officer	place
mouth	officers	play
move	old	playing
moved	older	pocket
movie	on	point
movies	once	pointed
Mr.	one	police
Mrs.	only	Porthos
much	open	Porthos's
Murphy	opened	pull
Murphy's	or	pulled
must	other	puppies
my	others	puppy
name	our	purse
named	out	put
near	outside	putting
nearly	over	quarter
need	own	quick
needed	owner	quiet
neighbor	owner's	quite
neighbors	package	rain

raincoat	she	stood
raining	show	stop
ran	showed	stopped
ready	shut	store
rest	sick	storm
restaurant	side	street
Rex	sister	streets
Rex's	sit	strong
ride	sitting	stuck
right	six	such
ring	sled	suddenly
river	sleep	sun
road	sleeping	Sunday
robber	sleepy	sure
robbers	slowly	surprised
robbery	smart	table
rocks	smell	tables
run	smelled	tail
running	smelling	take
Ruth	snow	taken
sacks	so	taking
said	some	talk
Saint Bernard	someone	talking
salmon	something	taught
sand	sometimes	tell
sat	soon	telling
saved	sound	ten
saw	speak	thank
say	stand	that
saying	standing	the
school	started	their
scratched	station	them
scruffy	stay	then
Scruffy's	stayed	there
see	stick	these
seemed	still	they
seen	stolen	things

think	used	where
thinks	very	whether
this	veterinarian	which
thought	voice	while
three	wagged	white
through	wagging	who
throw	wait	why
tied	waited	will
time	waiting	wind
to	waits	window
together	wake	windows
told	walk	winter
too	walked	with
took	walking	without
toward	want	woman
town	wanted	wonderful
toy	wanting	woods
toys	wants	Woof
track	warm	word
tracked	was	worked
train	watch	working
trained	watched	worn
trainer	watching	worth
tried	water	would
try	way	write
trying	we	yard
turned	weeks	years
two	well	yellow
until	went	yes
up	were	you
us	what	your
use	when